DAVID FICKLING AND PERRY HINTON
STARFLIGHT ZERO

```
PRIORITY   UNDER SEAL                           SUPREME COUNCIL ONLY

Sub V signal from PLNR 0026           Sigstation 037/17.98.10769

Partial vk jamming                    Comms. Officer Dacon 037/Co/4
Enhance failure


DARK SHIPS TOO STRONG FOR US ........... VAST ENEMY FLEET .........

F. P. SPACE FLEET CRUSHED ....... PLANET NOW DEFENCELESS ...... MERCILESS

BARRAGE OF OUR CITIES ........ CONTINENTS BURNING ....... DYING

PALACE DEFENCES FAILED ....... LAST MESSAGE ......... SIX SHIPS .........

REMAIN _ THE ROYAL FLIGHT ....... FLY TO OUR DOOM ........ THE KING HIMSELF

COMMANDS ........ BEYOND YOUR HELP ........ OUR WORLD ....... BLACK LIGHT

......... UPON US ........ REMEMBER ......... REMEMBER PALONAR .........
```

ILLUSTRATED BY
PETER ANDREW JONES

PUFFIN BOOKS

THE DARK SHIPS

The first 'Dark Ships' seen amongst the Free Planets struck terror into the hearts of those who saw them. Few survived to tell the tale, and those that did spread the rumour of a terrible weapon used by the invader – the 'Black Light'.

Lone space craft trading on the fringes would see sinister shapes looming on their forward scanners and turn to flee at maximum drive. The ship was rare that could outrun a raider – most didn't. The pilots were never seen again. Isolated settlements on remote planets would wake up to find the Dark Ships in their skies. The raiders came and destroyed installations, plundered minerals and materials and massacred or enslaved the population. Ships answering SOS calls would arrive to find nothing left of once thriving communities but the smoking ruins.

One by one the Free Planets began to fall to the invader. Nothing could withstand the full power of the Black Light. Those planets that surrendered had their populations shipped back to the enemy's home system. Those planets that refused were destroyed.

The war was a long one, taking many years. Desperately the scientists of the Free Planets searched for the source of the terrible power. They looked for a way to neutralize the Black Light and stem the evil tide. But remorselessly the enemy advanced until only two planets remained of the original twenty-three: Caldoran, the mother planet, and Palonar Royal, the glory of the Free Planets, a green jewel glittering in space . . .

Extract from **The Galactic History of the Free Planets**

The Council Meeting

Kal Dak, the leader of the Council, let fall the terrible signal and slumped down in his chair. He gazed at the tired faces around the table in the Supreme Council Chamber on Caldoran. The fall of Palonar has hit them hard, he realized. Many of the Council will now call for surrender.

Chief Scientist Galderin rose and began to speak quietly.

'We have identified the source of the Black Light.' The bald statement galvanized the meeting to attention. 'It is coming from a star on the other side of the galaxy, and is beamed directly from there to the enemy fleet. Their ships use it to destroy us in space battle. As you are aware, the Black Light breaks all known physical laws. The beam travels instantaneously across space. This is both its strength and its weakness. It enables the enemy to deploy its fleet anywhere in the galaxy.' The Scientist paused for effect. 'But if we can destroy the source, then the enemy fleet will be instantly helpless. Admiral?'

Galderin sat down. It was seconds before the Council realized what the Scientist had said. But Kal Dak grasped the significance with increasing excitement. He has given us a chance, he thought. We've got a chance.

Admiral Storth was already on his feet. A battle-scarred figure, he glared at his audience, defying them to countenance surrender. 'We propose to send a Starflight of eight ships across the galaxy to destroy the source of the Black Light. We have gathered together eight very different space fighters. They all share one priceless advantage amongst others. They are all fast. We believe they can outrun a Dark Ship. However, they are much smaller and carry nothing like the firepower. They will need the finest pilots we have. We have picked irregulars, but they can all fly like angels. Starflight Zero is ready to go at your order.'

The excitement around the table grew. Now they had a chance to fight back. But the jubilation was short lived.

'Are we all mad?' It was Zartin Klan of Tarelos. 'What is the Admiral suggesting? That we send eight puny craft across the breadth of the galaxy to destroy the enemy stronghold? The enemy's space fleets control the galaxy. Our fleet has been defeated. Our forces have been pushed back into one miserable solar system. Twenty-two of our planets have been utterly destroyed. We can no longer even travel to the nearest star, still less across the galaxy. The natural hazards of space would alone make such a mission foolhardy. In an enemy-controlled galaxy, it becomes impossible. And our Admiral proposes to do this with eight untried spacecraft and a bunch of "irregulars". We know what that means: petty space traders, shuttle pilots, aliens and such riff raff. The dregs of the twenty-three worlds or what is left of the dregs. No, I say we have no choice. Palonar was our last chance. Now we must throw ourselves on the mercy of the enemy. This is our only chance of survival. Better to be slaves than a cloud of forgotten dust in the universe.'

Kal Dak saw many heads around the table nodding in pained agreement as Zartin Klan sat down. They don't want to agree, but the logic is irrefutable, he thought. He found himself half agreeing. Nothing can stop the Black Light. All our efforts are doomed to failure.

One man stood up. He waited as the heads around the table came up. Kal Dak was astonished.

'Palonar has the floor,' he said.

The tension rose in the room. Finally, the Ambassador from Palonar, representing the last members of the oldest of the free races, spoke. He said only six words:

'Don't let Palonar die in vain.'

The tension broke. It was enough. A hubbub of talking began.

Kal Dak signalled for quiet. He knew the die was cast, the mood had changed. They would fight; surrender was unthinkable.

'Friends,' he said, 'the Ambassador from Palonar is right. We have work to do. I move that the Starflight Zero Mission is authorized.'

There were no dissenters.

Crew Data

LIEUTENANT JAN MARGOLLIN
Planet: Caldoran
Ship: **Nemesis**

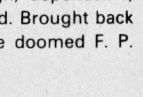

Human female (26). Starflight Leader. Tough, dependable, cynical, battle-hardened and very experienced. Brought back the only surviving space squadron from the doomed F. P. Starfighter Carrier *Orion*.

THE HONGRIN
Planet: Haath
Ship: **Small-Bird-That-Flies-Fast**

Alien. One of a mysterious Haathen order dedicated to preserving the life of the galaxy. Uncannily intuitive pilot. Knows the 'way of the stars', and can sense and control many of the natural dangers. Will avoid killing unnecessarily.

HARLEY YOUNGBACK
Planet: Domos
Ship: **Solar Roller**

Human male (16). Delinquent, rebellious mathematical prodigy. Built his own spaceship at the age of eleven. Potentially the greatest pilot of all time, but impulsive and inclined to show off.

ANCHORET RINN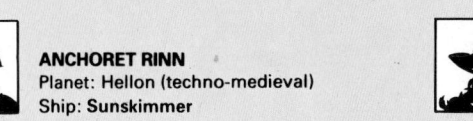
Planet: Hellon (techno-medieval)
Ship: **Sunskimmer**

Human female (20). From scientifically advanced, socially backward culture. Proud, honourable, dangerous. Probably the finest natural pilot on the Starflight. Three times winner of the lethal biennial Hellon 'Star Joust'.

THE SPACEHAWK
Planet: Unknown
Ship: **The Eurydice**

Elderly humanoid male (100 +). Vastly experienced trader/pirate/smuggler/scout/legendary figure. Very little is known about his origin. Great survivor. He and his ship are a legend throughout the galaxy.

KESTER JAX
Planet: Manash
Ship: **The Green Pearl**

Human male (33). Lonely, morose and crippled in space accidents. Only alive at the controls of his ship. A brilliant mining pilot. Only man to have made the legendary 'Long Run' for a green pearl of Calast ore *twice*.

BEM (Brain Emulator Droid)
Planet: Soramel
Ship: **ARC 1**

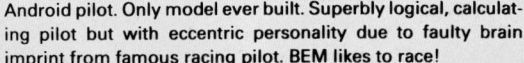

Android pilot. Only model ever built. Superbly logical, calculating pilot but with eccentric personality due to faulty brain imprint from famous racing pilot. BEM likes to race!

The Briefing

The small briefing room is stuffy. In front of you is the *Star Grid* on the wall-wide screen. The diminutive figure of Chief Scientist Galderin stands before you, speaking in his usual quietly animated manner. There are eight seats in the room. As you look at your fellow-members of the Starflight Zero, you realize that this is probably the greatest team of pilots ever gathered together in the history of the Free Planets. And YOU are one of them. You concentrate now on Galderin's words.

' . . . Our attack must be swift and the surprise complete. For this reason we shall not tell you even now the location of the enemy.'

You are as surprised as your fellow-pilots to hear this.

'We shall not tell *you*, but we shall tell your shipboard computers. The exact location of the enemy system and the pinpointed source of the Black Light (to an accuracy of one metre) have been fed into your computers. The computer will not reveal the source of the Black Light until you are in contact with the enemy base itself.

'The voyage to the enemy system has been divided into thirteen stages, or star sectors. As you complete each stage, the computer will ask you for a *Ship Status* report. This represents the condition of you and your ship. If you successfully complete the Ship Status for all thirteen star sectors of the voyage, then your ship's computer will reveal the source of the Black Light. Complete information on how to calculate your Ship Status is contained in the sealed orders and *Starflight Technical Data* that will be given to you after this briefing.'

Galderin pauses. 'Any questions?'

You realize that the time for questions is over. You glance at your fellow-pilots. They too are silent. Galderin looks round at a figure standing in the shadows.

'Admiral?'

Admiral Storth steps forward. His voice is crisp and businesslike. 'I have come here from the Supreme Council itself. The Starflight Zero Mission has been authorized. Few if any of you will return. The fate of the last Free Planet, and perhaps the future of the galaxy, is in your hands. The thoughts of millions are with you . . .'

Top Secret (For Pilot's Eyes Only)

SHIP'S CONTROLS

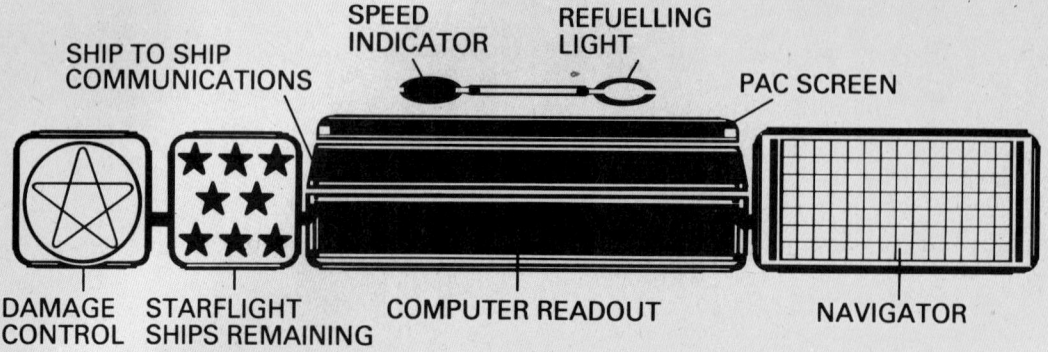

Study the controls and the space scene on each viewscreen carefully and obey the following instructions:

Galactic Co-ordinates

First you must work out your position. This is marked by a blue dot on each **Navigator** (see Controls Diagram). You must find this position on the **Star Grid** (see inside back cover). Read off the numbers for **Sub-Space** and **Hyper-Space** as shown on the Star Grid. Enter these numbers on your **Ship's Log** (inside front cover).

Damage Report

Look at your **Damage Control** (see Controls Diagram). If you have been hit by enemy fire or a meteor, this instrument will show any damage that your ship has suffered. A green section means no damage; an orange section means minor damage; and a red section means major damage. Refer to the **Starflight Technical Data** for the value of any damage caused. Add up the values and enter the total on your Ship's Log.

Danger Level

Study the viewscreen very carefully. How many enemy ships can you see? Identify the type of each enemy ship and find its **Danger Rating** in the Starflight Technical Data. Add up all the Danger Ratings of all enemy ships that can be identified on your viewscreen. This is the **Danger Level**. Enter this number on your Ship's Log.

Fuel

Your ship uses Liquid Calast as fuel for its Star Drive. You must calculate how much you have left.

Study your controls.

If the **Refuelling Light** is on, then your tanks are full and you have 50 units of Liquid Calast.

If the Refuelling Light is off, then you have used up fuel. Take your ship's speed from the **Speed Indicator**.

The **Speed/Fuel Table** in the Starflight Technical Data will tell you how much fuel you have used in this star sector. Subtract this number from the amount you had in the last sector for your present total. Enter this number on your Ship's Log.

Pilot Ability Check (PAC)

The ship's computer will also assess your ability to carry on with the mission. Read the question asked by the computer on the **PAC Screen**. The answer is a number. Enter this number on your Ship's Log.

You should now have six different numbers. If you have completed the Ship Status correctly, you will be able to retrieve part of the coded message.

Select the words from the **Computer Readout** that correspond to the numbers of the Ship Status (e.g. if the value for Sub-Space is 15, then take the fifteenth word). Do this for all the six numbers until you have six words. Write these words in the spaces provided in your Ship's Log.

As you complete the Ship Status for each stage of your mission, more and more of the computer message will be given to you. This message will instruct you on how to reveal the source of the Black Light.

YOUR ORDERS ARE TO DESTROY THIS SOURCE UTTERLY AND SO SAVE THE GALAXY FROM THE EVIL INVADERS

PAC: WHAT IS THE CALL

HALLKIN: WELCOME FRIENDS * I DID
MARGOLLIN: PALONAR IS LOST, PRINC
REVENGE * WELCOME TO THE STARFLI

* COLOUR SCAN OF PLANET PALONAR SHOW
SHIPS LOOT AND PLUNDER PLANET * ENEMY
THIS SECTOR OF THE GALAXY * ALL SIGN
UNKNOWN CRAFT ATTACKING DARK SHIPS *
INDICATES A PALONARIAN NAVAL VESSEL
PALONARIAN NOBLE HOUSE HALLKIN * SH
FLIGHT OF PALONAR * PRINCESS LARA HA

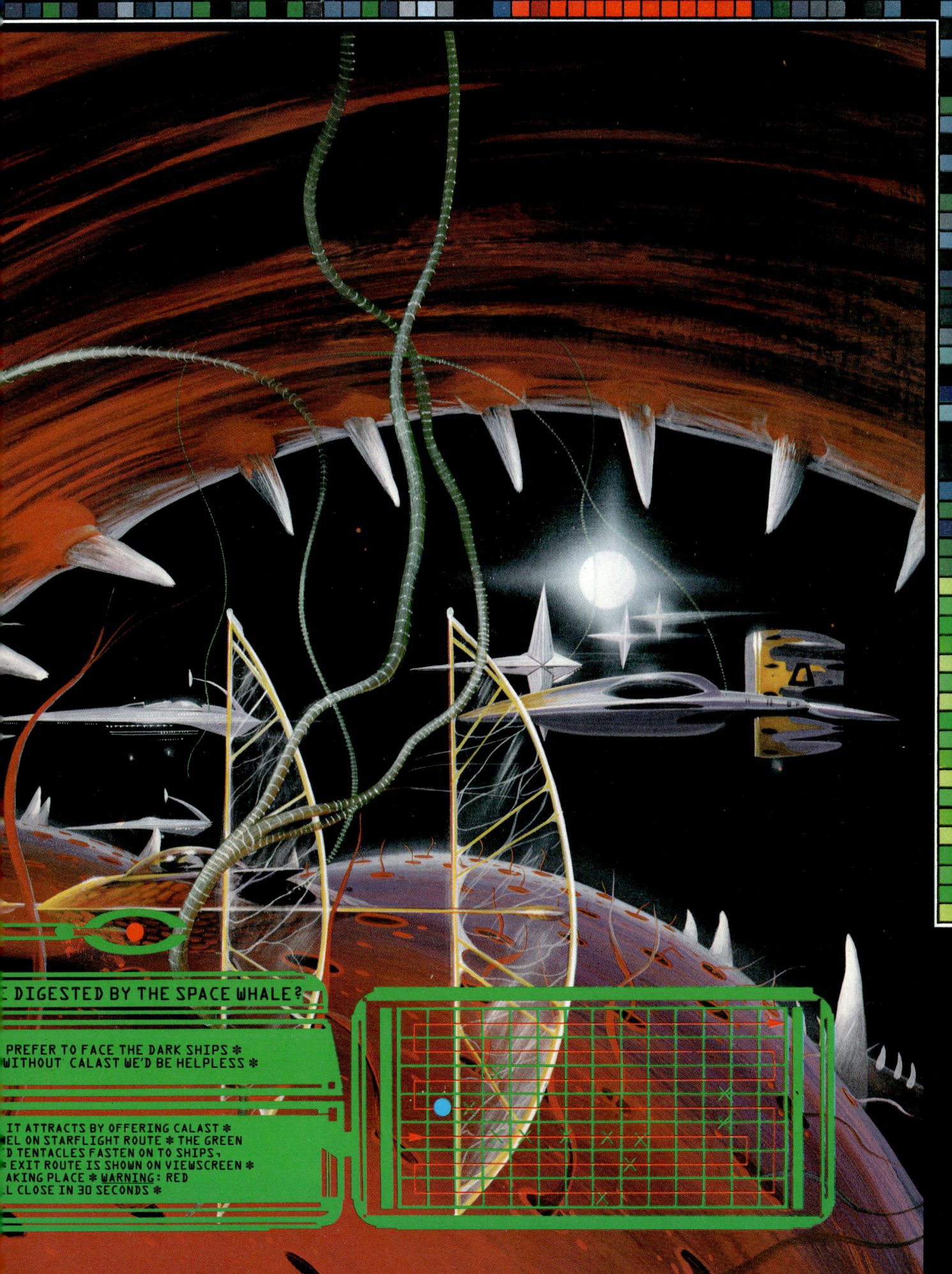

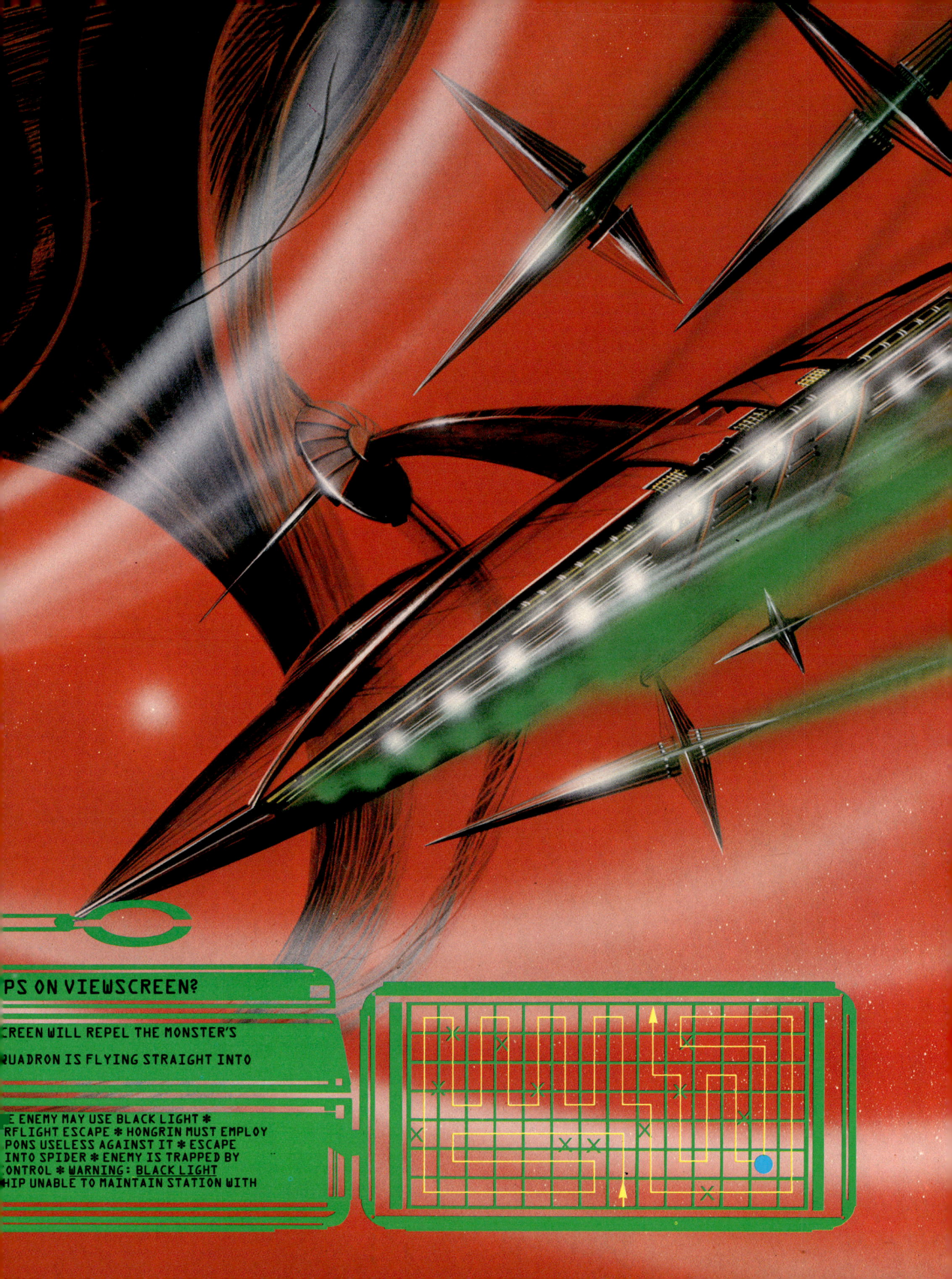

STARFLIGHT TECHNICAL DATA

DARK SHIPS

Star Dagger class ship
Danger Rating **2**

Star Hammer class ship
Danger Rating **4**

Star Crusher class ship
Danger Rating **6**

Cargo ship
Danger Rating **3**

Troop carrier
Danger Rating **2**

Supernova class ship
Danger Rating **35**

Disabled Dark Ships of any class have a Danger Rating of **1**

The total Danger Rating of the Dark Towers is **45**

DAMAGE CONTROL VALUES

Minor damage   Major damage

No damage   Example: Total damage value = **11**

SPEED/FUEL TABLE

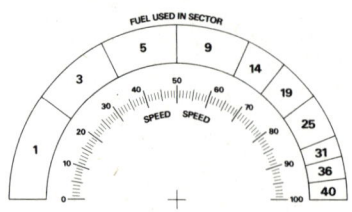

Line up cross with speed and read off fuel used in sector (Example: A speed of 55 will give 9 units of fuel used in the sector)

SHIPS OF STARFLIGHT ZERO

The Eurydice 1
Pilot: Spacehawk
Converted trading craft

Starbolt 2
Pilot: YOU
Experimental prototype

Solar Roller 3
Pilot: Harley Youngback
Souped-up speedster

The Green Pearl 4
Pilot: Kester Jax
Converted asteroid mining craft

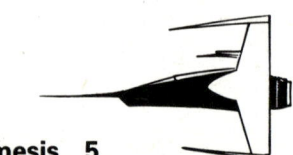

Nemesis 5
Pilot: Lieutenant Jan Margollin
Converted F. P. Navy fighter

ARC 1 6
Pilot: BEM
Converted racing ship

Small-Bird-That-Flies-Fast 7
Pilot: The Hongrin
Organic craft. Mental control system

Sunskimmer 8
Pilot: Anchoret Rinn
Converted jousting vessel

Puffin Books, Penguin Books Ltd, Harmondsworth, Middlesex, England
Viking Penguin Inc., 40 West 23rd Street, New York, New York 10010, U.S.A.
Penguin Books Australia Ltd, Ringwood, Victoria, Australia
Penguin Books Canada Ltd, 2801 John Street, Markham, Ontario, Canada L3R 1B4
Penguin Books (N.Z.) Ltd, 182–190 Wairau Road, Auckland 10, New Zealand

First published 1985

Copyright © David Fickling and Perry Hinton, 1985
Illustrations copyright © Peter Andrew Jones, 1985
All rights reserved

Made and printed in Great Britain by
Hazell Watson & Viney Ltd, Aylesbury
Member of the BPCC Group,
Aylesbury, Bucks

Filmset in Univers (Linotron 202) by
Rowland Phototypesetting Ltd,
Bury St Edmunds, Suffolk

Except in the United States of America, this book is sold subject to the condition that it shall not, by way of trade or otherwise, be lent, re-sold, hired out, or otherwise circulated without the publisher's prior consent in any form of binding or cover other than that in which it is published and without a similar condition including this condition being imposed on the subsequent purchaser